NAME
FOR THE
CORNISH

THREE HUNDRED
CORNISH
CHRISTIAN NAMES

© 1984 Dyllansow Truran

Published by Dyllansow Truran, Croft Prince,
Mount Hawke, Truro, Cornwall TR4 8EE

Distributed by Tor Mark, Islington Wharf,
Penryn, Cornwall TR10 8AT

Printed in Great Britain by
Short Run Press Ltd, Exeter

ISBN 0 907566 94 4

INTRODUCTION

This booklet has been prepared to help Cornish parents with the practical business of choosing distinctively Cornish christian names for their children. That there are parents who have considered giving their son or daughter a Cornish name is apparent from the steady flow of spontaneous inquiries which have been received over the years, the past few years especially, by people who are connected in one way or another with the Cornish cultural and historical societies. Most inquirers have asked for a comprehensive list of Cornish names, and have been surprised and disappointed when told that no such list exists. This booklet, containing over 300 names, represents an attempt to meet this demand.

The upsurge of interest in Cornwall's native names, and in names with Cornish associations, seems to be the natural accompaniment of a growing Cornish awareness of the distinctiveness of Cornwall's cultural background. It seems to be related, too, to the readiness of modern parents to make use of newly - coined and revived names, which is perhaps the most marked trend to emerge in christian name selection in this century. There are probably more christian names in use in Britain today than at any other time since the early 13th century.

The modern revival of disused names began in the 18th century, which saw the resurrection of the Old English names like EDGAR, EDWIN and ALFRED. Some of these names had been absolete for the better part of six centuries. The fashion accelerated in the 19th century, when a host of old-fashioned and long-obsolete names came back into use as a result of the efforts of the various religious and literary movements of the time. Names like WILFRID, HAROLD, AMY, ROGER, HUGH and GUY are now so firmly re-established that few people realise that they are essentially revived names. The fashion has continued ever since, every decade or so restoring to favour a fresh crop of obsolete or unfashionable names. There is no reason whatever why the pleasant-sounding names of the Cornish past - names like TALAN, PERAN, ELWYN, ERVAN, KENVER and KENWYN - should not share in this fashion.

The Norman Conquest had a deep and lasting influence on the christian names and surnames of future generations of Cornishmen. It came only a century of so after Cornwall's annexation by England, and at a time when the vast majority of Cornish people bore native Celtic names. These, described throughout this booklet as Old Cornish, derived from names current among the Britons before the English advance westwards confined most of them to Wales and Cornwall, and encouraged others to found a new colony in what is now Brittany. Not all of these names went back to a pristine Celtic source; many of them had been borrowed from the Romans by their forbears during the occupation period, and had become absorbed into the British language, the ancestor of Welsh, Cornish and Breton.

Although there seems to be no documentary evidence which points to a rapid decline in the use of the Old Cornish names in post - Conquest Cornwall, the speed with which Old English names gave way to the newly-introduced Norman names may give some indication of what happened in Cornwall. East of the Tamar, where the majority of the population bore Old English names, the abandonment of the old names in favour of the new was virtually completed within two centuries. Among the English upper classes, Old English names disappeared within two or three generations. They may have survived rather longer among the peasantry, but by the end of the 13th century very few peasants went by Old English names. Out of 800 jurors and bailiffs in the Eyre of Kent, 1313-14, only seven bore Old English names. Norman-introduced names dominate the records of the period. Apart from the flood of WILLIAMS, WALTERS, RICHARDS, ROBERTS, RALPHS, ODOS and HUGHS, the Normans also brought with them a number of names of Breton origin, among them IVES, SAMPSON and ALAN.

The Old Cornish secular names seem to have vanished in the same way under this vast overburden of Norman names. When we encounter a Cornishman in a 12th century or 13th century document, the chances are that we find him bearing one of the four most popular names of the period, WILLIAM, RALPH and RICHARD, which together accounted for about 44% of the male population. The christian names occuring in the 1327 Lay Subsidy Rolls for the western half of Cornwall merely reflect contemporary fashions in names, with JOHN - as elsewhere - naming about 25% of Cornish males. Yet it seems possible that a few Old Cornish secular names may have lingered on in use among the Cornish-speaking peasantry and were never recorded. So much of the extant documentation of early medieval Cornwall is concerned with the Anglo-Norman ruling class, with non-Cornish clerics, and with the predominantly non-Cornish townsfolk.

It is perhaps never wise to jump to the conclusion that the few Celtic names which occur in early post-Conquest sources are indigenous names, for they are nearly always indistinguishable from Breton names, and could have been re-introduced into Cornwall by Breton followers of the Conqueror who were given Cornish estates, or by the later wave of Breton labourers, artisans and curates who settled in Cornwall. Sometimes the social status of the bearer provides a clue.

Cornish Celtic surnames, most of which are regarded as having come into existence between 1250 and 1450, are derived from place-names, nicknames, occupational names, or have a characteristically Cornish appearance but are otherwise unidentifiable. The great majority belong to the place-name category. Among the English peasantry, the Old English uncompounded names seem to have outlived the compounded ones, and

4

are thought to account for a number of English surnames. It is conceivable (whether or not it is likely is another matter) that some Old Cornish names, perhaps the uncompounded ones, survived long enough to give rise to surnames. Rather unflattering surnames like MOYLE, "bald", are patently nickname surnames and nothing more, but surnames like TALLACK, believed to represent the Cornish adjective TALEK, "big-browed", seem possible as Old Cornish first-names. Cf. the Bodmin Manumissions names FRIOC and TALAN, both of which are listed. GWYNNOW (cf. the Old Breton name UUINOU), PENNECK, MYNNOW, MELOWARN and WENAN are other rare or obsolete Cornish surnames which may possibly derive from Old Cornish first-names.

The Cornish play BEWNANS MERYASEK demonstrates that the Old Cornish names of some traditional Cornish kings were still remembered - though not used as christian names, of course - in the late 15th century, five hundred years after the annexation of Cornwall. (See page 24 for a description of the play). The fact that they were remembered at all has its significance, for the few Old English names retained by post - Conquest Englishman invariably fell into two categories; either they were the names of saints (e.g. EDMUND) or they were the names of former kings of the house of Wessex (e.g. EDGAR).

There are apparently no records of the use of the names of the Cornish petty kings as christian names, but the tradition of naming children after a Cornish saint survived up to the beginning of the 19th century. Indeed, the last flicker of the tradition has still not been extinguished, for MORWENNA is still used as a name for Cornish girls. PERAN, PETROK, GERENS and MAWGAN are only a few of the Cornish saints' names which past generations of Cornishmen adopted as christian names. The earlier parish registers suggest that although it was perhaps more usual for a child to take the name of the saint of his own parish, this was not an invariable rule.

The names of the better-known saints, PETROK and GERENS for example, seem to have had a fairly wide distribution in western and central Cornwall. Occasionally the saint's name was given a feminine form (e.g. COLUMBA for COLUM) to make it suitable for bestowal on girls, but it is not certain that the change in form meant that the name was pronounced differently. It is possible that the difference was a written one only, like the use of PHILIPPA for girls who were actually called PHILIP. The decline in the use of the names of the Cornish saints seem to date from the Reformation, when all of the non-scriptural saints' names became unfashionable. They become much rarer in Cornish parish registers after the first half of the 17th century, but are still found from time to time in the early 18th century.

With the exception of the names of the Cornish saints and a few secular and semi-secular names like PASCOW, the only other native names to survive were the Cornish forms of certain scriptural names (e.g. JOWAN for English "John"), nearly all of which are found only in Cornish literary sources. Because of the language's lack of legal status and low social standing, such names are invariably given their standard Latin or English forms in official documents and the earlier parish registers.

Pet-names (i.e. WILL for "William") have a distinctive history in Cornwall. When the Cornish borrowed a word from Middle English they invariably retained the now-silent final "e" formerly sounded in many English words, or added their own final "a" if the word did not end in a vowel. Cf. the Cornish word DAMA with English "dame". This seems to account for a group of A-suffix pet-names like WELLA ("Will"), HICCA ("Hick"/"Dick") and JACCA ("Jack") which flourished in Cornwall after the final "e" had ceased to be sounded in English words. There seems to be little doubt that from the 13th to 15th centuries the majority of Cornish agriculturists, fishermen and tinners went by these and similar pet-names. They occur from time to time in Cornish field names such as PARK JACCA and PARK HECCA, "Jack's field"/"Dick's field." It is interesting to find that as time went by HICCA and WELLA came to be regarded as distinctively Cornish. William Rowe of Sancreed, for example, a late 17th century translator into Cornish of parts of the Bible, liked to cornicize his name as WELLA KEREW.

Cornwall's O-suffix names have been the subject of a good deal of discussion. It is generally held (and by the late R. Morton Nance in particular) that the Cornish suffix -O/-OW does not correspond to the Breton diminutive suffix-OU or the Welsh diminutive suffix-O. Instead it is said to have the meaning "of", "of (the family", or " the son) of". This means that with the exception of PASCOW (JAGO is a name in its own right), all Cornish O-suffix names are essentially surnames, the -O/-OW suffix corresponding in function to the Middle English genitive singular inflexion -ES found in surnames like ANDREWES "(son) of Andrew". Whatever the real significance of the -O/-OW suffix, the Cornish historian Carew (1555-1620) gives CLEMMOWE as a Cornish first-name equivalent of standard English CLEMENCE/CLEMENT. Moreover, some O-suffix names are found used as christian names at a time when the custom of using surnames as christian names was rare outside the ranks of the gentry. There seems to be no reason why these names should not be included in this purely practical booklet.

Cornwall's prominence in the dictionaries of christian names springs from the fact that past generations of Cornishmen were slow to respond to fashions in christian names. They preferred to cultivate the old favourites of the Middle Ages, many of which lingered on in Cornish use long after their disappearance elsewhere. MARIOT, for example, the usual diminutive of MARY in the Middle Ages, was still in use in 18th century

6

Cornwall. REMFRY, too, practically absolete elsewhere since the 16th century, still survived in Cornwall in the last century. In its standard form RENFRED it still survives.

Then there are a number which have always been primarily Cornish when used in Britain; exotic names like the mainly Italian HANNIBAL. Finally, there is JENIFER, Cornish-reared, and now the ninth most popular name for girls in Britain.

The names selected for this booklet fall into the following categories:
(a) The names of Cornish saints, whether the saints were of Cornish, Breton, Welsh or Irish origin. (It should be borne in mind that the Cornish, Bretons and Welsh were virtually one people in The Age of the Saints). The list is not comprehensive. It excludes saints with a European-wide cult, certain saints whose gender is uncertain, and a few saints who are no more than "bare names" and probably highly corrupt names at that.
(b) The Cornish forms of certain scriptural names.
(c) The few Celtic secular names found in Cornish literature.
(d) The very small group of native names which still survive, or have only become obsolete in the past few centuries.
(e) Non-Celtic names which are associated with Cornwall and can be regarded as Cornish by adoption.
(f) A selection of obsolete non-Celtic names which were never peculiar to the Cornish, but which survived longer in Cornwall than in most other areas. This selection could have been expanded to include a host of archaic names; this would have defeated the object of this booklet, which is to supply distinguishingly Cornish names. Moreover, many of the obsolete names of the Middle Ages are merely early forms of modern names, or are so lacking in euphony as to be unacceptable to modern parents. This applies particularly to the medieval girls' names, many of which have an epicene, almost masculine appearance. BEATEN would have been excluded but for the fact that it ranks high on Cornwall's list of late survivors.
(g) A selection of O-suffix names.
(h) A selection of A-suffix names.
(i) Names taken from a Cornish dictionary in an effort to make good the shortage of girls' names. A few compound names defy the laws of normal Cornish usage in the greater interests of euphony and pronouncability.
(j) Respelt Old Cornish names. Unlike the Welsh and Irish, the Cornish do not possess an ancient secular literature in their language. Although no connected piece of Old Cornish writing has survived, a copious 12th century vocabulary supplies a good deal of information about the language at this stage of its development. Extant Middle Cornish literature (dating from the late 14th century) is devoted to religious themes and contains few secular names. The Welsh, on the other hand, have a rich and

...hoc liberauit ... p[ro]scen p[ro]pria sua sup[er] al...
... sci petroci cora[m] istis testibus ...
... diaconus canguethen ...
... clericus et aliis mult[is] ...

pulppre ep[iscopu]s liberauit aedoc filiam cat...
sua ... n[...] sup[er] altare sci petroci ...
... et ... in ...
... et uanop[re]c et pendeg[...] et purud ... in c[...]
et inipian et b[...]nci et on ... et ...
hec sunt nomina illorum hominum illa quin[que]
quos liberauit pulp[...]ge ep[iscopu]s sup[er] altare
sci petroci p[ro] anima sua et p[ro] no[...]mine euorc[...]

It hec s[un]t nomina illaru[m] feminaru[m] quas liberauit erm[...]
p[ro] anima ma[tris] illius idest gwengu[...] et elisaued cora[m] istis
testibus f[...]oc p[resbite]r et osiam p[resbite]r et leucum monachus.
hoc e[st] nom[en] illius hominis qui liberauit offend p[ro] anima
... regis et urher[...] sup[er] altare sci petroci cora[m]
istis testibus comoere piscopus azusanus lecto[r]
b[er]thsie sacerdos.
hec e[st] nom[en] qui liberauit eusebi p[ro] anima sua ce en zuled
sup[er] altare sci petroci cora[m] istis testib[us] g[...]sfuid legmanh
riol.
It hec s[un]t nomina illoru[m] hominu[m] quos liberauit anaoe giani[...]
ma sua et cer rannoeu muel patrec iosep sup[er] altare
... tan sacerdos leucum clericus guaed ... clericus
... s[an]c[t] ... nomina illoru[m] hominu[m] azustin aelchon ...
loi imb[...]nos zuennerec zurcencor riol anau[...]
euicen zurcant cest emud oncenedl lucco[...]
iudhen...

Opposite P. 141a of the Bodmin Manumissions, which occur in a manuscript generally called "The Bodmin Gospels", or "The St. Petrock Gospels", formerly the property of Bodmin Priory and now in the British Museum (Add. MS.9381). It was written at Bodmin at the beginning of the 10th century and contains a number of Latin and English marginal notes belonging to the 10th to 12th century, the great majority to the second half of the 10th century. These notes record the manumission of slaves at the Altar of St. Petrock and take the form, to quote a typical specimen: "This is the name of that man whom Cenmenoc liberated for his own soul on the altar of St. Petroc, Benedic, before these beholding witnesses, Osian, the priest, and Morhaitho, the deacon".

Of the 33 Manumittors, 24 have English names, 5 have Cornish names, and 4 have names of Graeco-Latin derivation. Among the manumitted slaves, on the other hand, there are 98 Cornish names, 12 Latin or Biblical names, and only 12 English names. In addition, there are the names of over a hundred witnesses, about half of whom bear Cornish names. It is probably that the Biblical names were borne by Cornishmen, for such names were rare among 10th century Englishmen. JOSEPH, a Manumission name, occurs only twice in an English context as a pre-Conquest christian name, and almost certainly names a Cornishman. One interesting feature of the Bodmin Manumissions is the apparent use by two Cornishmen (one a Bishop of Cornwall) of two names, an English one followed by a Cornish one.

The opposite page contains ten of the Old Cornish names listed in the booklet. With the exception of GRIFIUD and possibly WENDEERN, all seem to occur as elements in Cornish place-names. They are in order of occurence:-

CUSTENTIN (Costentyn) The Cornish form of CONSTANTINE
RIOL (Ryel/Ryol) Occurs in the play "Bewnans Meryasek".
RUMUN Also the name-saint of Ruan Lanihorne.
WENDEERN (Gwendern) Possibly the name saint of Wendron.

WURDYLIC (Gorthelyk)
BRENCI (Brengy)

FREOC (Fryek/Fryok)
GURHETER (Gorheder)

GRIFIUD (Grifyuth)
GURCANT (Gorgans)

---

ancient literature which is sufficiently early to contain scores of Old Welsh names which are found in Cornwall in their cognate Old Cornish forms only as names in the Bodmin Manumissions or as elements in place-names.

The Bodmin Manumissions record the manumission or freeing of Cornish slaves in the 10th and 11th centuries (see above for a fuller description), and contain 152 Celtic first-names, many of which are found

9

as place-name elements as well. A typical example is the name BRENCI, with the "c" pronounced as a "g". The name seems to occur in at least three Cornish place-names; in TREFINGEY, TRERINGEY and TREVINGEY, all of which once had the form TREVRENGY, "homestead (of) Brengy". (The mutation of the initial consonant of a name like BRENGY after TRE "homestead" is a regular feature of Cornish). As with most Cornish place-names, the early spellings of the three place-names in question are the only ones to be relied on. Some of the Bodmin Manumissions names, principally those which also occur in place-names, have been included in this booklet, but many more have been excluded on the grounds that they would have to be given a drastically altered appearance to bring them into line with the later stage of the language. These names have been analysed by Celtic scholars ranging from Whitely Stokes to Förster, and while most of them could be reconstructed on Middle Cornish lines, it has been felt unnecessary to go to these lengths in a booklet limited to supplying three hundred names drawn from all sources. In most cases it has been felt preferable to select "ready-made Middle Cornish" names which occur in Cornwall only as place-name elements, but which are backed by Welsh and/or Breton cognate names. Far more importance has been attached to a name's Welsh and/or Breton pedigree than to the certainly or near certainty that the name is found in Cornish place-names. Only a very few place-names can be interpreted with absolute certainty; in most cases they can only be interpreted with a greater or lesser degree of probability. In this booklet these names have been allowed to remain, subject to certain modifications, in the form in which they occur in medieval spellings of place-names approximately west of a line drawn from Padstow to Fowey.

In this area, most of which was Cornish-speaking throughout the Middle Ages, the majority of place-names were as much a part of the contemporary language as the English place-name LONG LANE, which no one would dream of spelling as LANG LONE or corrupting as LOLLAN. The meanings of most place-names must have been familiar to Cornish-speakers, for the elements they contained (e.g. NANS, TRE, COS) were part of the living, evolving language. Once the names ceased to have real meanings for those who used them, and became "just names", the spellings became subject to much variation and corruption. Although there is no way of establishing whether the Celtic names attached to familiar place-name elements were perceived as obsolete names by medieval Cornishmen or whether they were "just names", they shared in the transition from Old Cornish to Middle Cornish, and usually appear in the form that they would have had if they had continued to be used as names. The etymologies given are based on the best information available to the compiler, which is not the same as saying that it is the most up-to-date information available to specialists in this field. The important thing is that they exist as names; their bearers were as oblivious or ignorant (if

10

Old English names are any guide) of their meanings as modern bearers of the name ALFRED. The usual asterisks marking hypothetical British linguistic forms are dispensed with in this purely practical booklet.

The names of some of the Celtic saints have come down to us little affected by the passage of time, while the names of others survive in varying degrees of mutilation. Some (e.g. CARANTOC) are found only in their Old Cornish form; others (e.g. MERIADOC/MERYASEK) are known in their later form as well. The transition in spelling from Old Cornish -OC to Middle Cornish -EK reflected the change in the accentuation of Cornish words which was completed by or during the 11th century. Hitherto, the accent had been placed on the ultimate syllable, as it still is in the "fossilized" saints' names ending in -OC. The new accent, which fell on the penultimate syllable (e.g. Mer-YAS-ek), is familiar to most people through Cornish place-names. (At about the same time -LT, - NT became - LS, -NS; and -D, -T became S, pronounced Z). No attempt has been made to transform Old Cornish saints' names into Middle Cornish ones (e.g. to turn CARANTOC into CARANSEK or something similar), since this would be going too far. But the opportunity has been taken to cornicize some spellings on later lines, and to repair some of the ravages of time and anglicization. For example, some "fossilized" names like WINWALOE have remained immune to the development of British initial U (i.e. W) to GW-. Although this change had taken place by the 10th century, orthographic traditionalism ensured the survival of U, etc., right down to the end of the Old Cornish period. The place-name GUNWALLOE (earlier GWYNWALLA), named after the saint, reflects this change, and in this booklet WINWALOE is found as GWYNWALLO(W). In many cases conflicts between Old Cornish and later Cornish forms are resolved by giving both, e.g. BUTHEK/BUDOK, the Middle Cornish form (or less anglicized form in the case of Buthek/Budok) taking precedence.

SPELLING

The aim has been to keep a middle course. As far as possible, all Celtic names are spelt in accordance with Middle Cornish principles, but this aim has not been followed blindly, especially when it has seemed likely to lessen the attractiveness of a name for modern users. In general, saints' names are given their more Cornish medieval spellings. The Old Cornish -OC in names like Petroc has given way to -OK for three reasons. The first of these is that -Oc is used in the anglicized rendering of Welsh names ending in - OG; the second is that final -C has been foreign to Cornish spelling since the Old Cornish period; and the third is that final -C has an archaic (or Welsh) appearance. THE SPELLINGS ARE SUGGESTED ONES ONLY, for there are no hard-and-fast conventions governing the spelling of Cornish names. It is better for names like PETROK to be anglicized as

11

PETROCK (the usual spelling adopted by earlier generations of users) than not used at all. If parents dislike the appearance of the Y retained in some Cornish names, they are at liberty to use a more modern I. Some may prefer to use a Z in place of an S in a Cornish name, bearing in mind that, except when initial, a Cornish S is invariably pronounced Z.

Professional students of the Celtic languages, Cornish historians, hagiologists and other specialists are reminded of the title of this booklet; it sets out to provide NAMES FOR THE CORNISH - nothing more. While every care has been taken in the compilation of the list, inconsistencies and questionable etymologies are bound to have crept in.

ACKNOWLEDGEMENTS

I am indebted to the late Mr. Richard Blewett, of St. Day, for making available his analysis of first-names occurring in the 1327 Lay Subsidy Rolls for the Hundreds of western and central Cornwall, and to Mr. H.L. Douch, of the Royal Institution of Cornwall, for permission to reproduce pages 95 and 98 of the Institution's photostat copy of the play "Bewnans Meryasek".

A NOTE ON PRONUNCIATION

The stress or accent in a Cornish word of two syllables is normally put on that before the last, as in Cornish place-names. The "imitated pronunciation" used in the list indicates stress by the use of capital letters. For example, the place-name TRENOWETH would be rendered "Tre-NOW-eth". When a word is not accompanied by its "imitated pronunciation," it may be assumed that it is pronounced like a similarly spelt English word. EXCEPT WHEN INITIAL, and in the combination, SS, S in CORNISH NAMES has the SOUND OF Z.

SYMBOLS & ABBREVIATIONS

+	preceding a name indicates that it cannot be regarded as distinguishingly Cornish.
D	indicates that a name is not traditional and that it has been taken from a Cornish dictionary.
PN	the capital letters PN indicate that a respelt Old Cornish name seems to be found as a place-name element, but that it does not seem to be attested in other sources.
RS	= respelt and occurs in phrases like "RS Old Cornish name". (It was felt that it would be misleading to describe such names as bare "Old Cornish" names).
=	this symbol is used for "the equivalent of", "corresponding to", "cognate with", "the same as", etc.

Bod. Man. = Bodmin Manumissions.

NAMES OF BOYS

+ALAN
A Celtic name of doubtful etymology. The name of an obscure Breton saint who gave his name to St. Allen, near Truro, ALAN was introduced into England as whole by Breton followers of William the Conqueror. ALAN has since become so common that its connection with Cornwall is usually overlooked. The spellings ALLAN and ALLEN are not supported by Breton and early Cornish tradition.

ALWAR
(Pron. "al-WORE") The name of a traditional Cornish king in the play "Bewnans Meryasek", but apparently not an Old Cornish name at all. It is probably the Old English name AELFWARU which Eilert Ekwall (Oxford Dictionary of English Place-Names) sees in the Madron place-name ALVERTON (ALWARTON 1229), "Alwar's homestead".

ARTHEK
PN A RS Old Cornish name = the Old Welsh name ARTHWG, a derivative of ARTH, "bear".

+ARTHUR
The name of the semi-historical British freedom fighter who has a special place in the memory of the Cornish. The etymology of the name has been the subject of much dispute; it may be derived from British ARTOS, "bear", but is more probably of Latin origin. Like ALAN, ARTHUR is too common to be distinguishingly Cornish.

ARTHYEN
PN A RS Old Cornish name = the Old Welsh name ARTHIEN, from British ARCTOGENOS, "bear born".

AUSTOL
A Breton saint who gave his name to St. Austell.

+BASTIAN
Latin SEBASTIANUS, "man of Sebastia" (a city). A shortened form of SEBASTIAN not uncommon in 16th century Cornwall. Essentially a French and Spanish name.

+BAWDEN or BOWDEN
Old German BALDAVIN, a compound of BALDA, "bold", and VINI, "friend". BAWDEN, fairly common in Cornwall up to the 17th century, is from BAUDOIN, the Norman-French form of BALDWIN.

BENESEK
(Pron. "be-NEZZ-ek") A RS Old Cornish name from Latin BENEDICTUS, "blessed", found as a Bod. Man. name and as a possible place-name element.

BRANEK or BRANOK
PN A RS Old Cornish name found in a number of place-names.

BRANWALATHER
(Pron. "bran-wol-LATH-er") Some authorities believe that St. Branwalather, about whom nothing is known, is honoured at St. Breward. The name means "raven leader".

BRENGY
(Pron. "brenn-gee") A RS Old Cornish name found in the Bod. Man. and as an element in several place-names. The name means "noble dog".

BRYOK or BREOK
(Pron. "bree-OK") A Welsh saint who gave his name to St. Brieuc in Brittany and to St. Breock in Cornwall. The name is from British BRIGACOS.

BUTHEK, BITHEK, or BUDOK
(Pron. The "th" like the soft "th" in "that") A Breton saint who gave his name to the parish of Budock, near Falmouth. BUDOC(K) is the anglicized Old Cornish form of the name, which occurs in its Middle Cornish form BUTHEK, in medieval sources and is partly preserved in the surname BIDDICK. BITHEK is a suggested spelling with modern use in mind. BUTHEK, which means "victorious", is the masculine form of the name of the famous Queen Budhycca (Boadicea) who led a revolt against the Romans. The name occurs in the Bod. Man.

CADAN
PN A RS Old Cornish name = the Old Welsh name CADAN

CADRETH
PN A RS Old Cornish name = the Old Welsh name CADREITH.

CADOR
A legendary ruler of Cornwall. Old Cornish CADWUR, "warrior".

CARANTOK
(Pron. "car-RANT-OK") A Welsh saint who gave his name to Crantock, near Newquay, and to several other places in Wales and Brittany. The names seems to be a derivative of the root CARANT, "love".

14

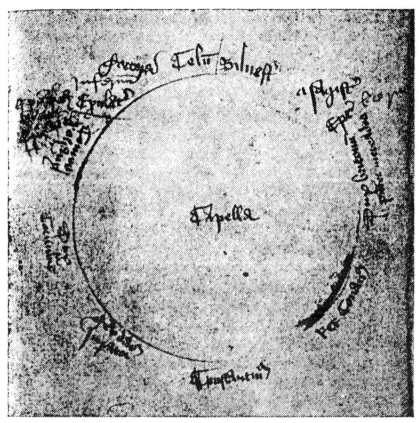

BEWNANS MERYASEK — the stage plan for the second day

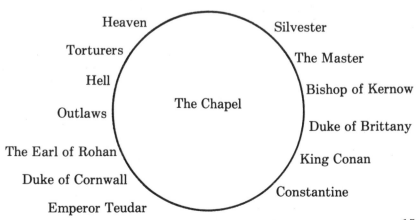

Heaven

Torturers

Hell

Outlaws

The Earl of Rohan

Duke of Cornwall

Emperor Teudar

The Chapel

Silvester

The Master

Bishop of Kernow

Duke of Brittany

King Conan

Constantine

15

CARASEK or **CARADOK**
(Pron. "car-RAZZ-ek"/"car-RADD-OK") The name of a legendary Duke of Cornwall and of a famous chieftain, Caractacus, who was taken to Rome as a prisoner in the 1st century A.D. The name means "amiable". Since CARADWG is a favourite christian name in Wales, there is everything to be said for preferring CARASEK, the distinctively Cornish medieval place-name form of the name.

CASEK or **CADOK**
(Pron. "cazz-ek"/"cadd-OK") A common place-name element. St. Cadoc, one of the most famous of Welsh saints, may have visited Cornwall, where the well-known chapel at Harlyn Bay bears his name. Middle Cornish CASEK is more "Cornish" and is unlikely to be confused with Welsh CADOG.

CASVELYN
(Pron. "caz-VELL-an") Found as the name of a traditional Cornish petty king in the play "Bewnans Meryasek". A native Celtic name, it may derive from British CATU-BELINUS.

CASWAL
(Pron. "cazz-woll") A RS Old Cornish name meaning "battle powerful".

CASWORON
PN (Pron. "cazz-WORR-an" - rhymes with the place-name "Gorran") A RS Old Cornish name meaning "battle hero".

CASWYN
PN (Pron. "cazz-win") A RS Old Cornish name from British CATU-UINDOS, "fair battle".

CATHNO(W)
PN (Pron. "cath-noo") A RS Old Cornish name = the Old Welsh name CADNOU, "battle-known".

CLEMO(W)
(Pron. "clemm-O") A Cornish O-suffix pet-form of CLEMENT. The Cornish historian Carew (1555-1620) gives CLEMMOWE as the Cornish first-name equivalent of standard English CLEMENCE/CLEMENT.

CLESEK
PN (Pron. "clezz-ek") A RS Old Cornish name = the Old Welsh name CLODOC, from British KLUTO-, "famous".

CLETHER
(Pron. to rhyme with "leather") Apart from the appearance of his name in the Cornish list of the Children of Brychan, nothing is known about the saint who gave his name to St. Clether in Cornwall and to Cleder in Brittany.

COLAN
(Pron. to rhyme with "pollen". A Celtic saint who gave his name to Colan, near Newquay. He is probably the saint whose name is perpetuated in Llangollen in Wales and in Langolen in Brittany. As a Cornish christian name, COLAN is found up the end of the 17th century.

COLUM
(Pron. "cull-um") A Celtic missionary who, despite tradition to the contrary, was probably a man. The name, like Irish COLUM/COLM, is from Latin COLUMBA, "dove". Used up to 1610 as a name for boys born in the parish of St. Columb, but also found later elsewhere.

CONAN
(Pron. "conn-an" and *not* like the name of the author, Conan Doyle) The name of a semi-historical Cornish king and of an authentic 10th century Bishop of Cornwall. A fairly common place-name element and possibly the real name of the patron of Roche, St. Gonand. CONAN = Old Welsh CYNAN, Old Breton CONAN and Irish CONAN. The name still survives in Brittany, and owes its survival in Britain to its post-Conquest reintroduction by Breton settlers. Fairly common from the 12th to 16th centuries. For a form of the name unlikely to be regarded as an English name, see KENAN.

CORENTYN
(Pron. "cawr-RENT-in") A Breton saint, honoured as first bishop of Cornouaille and associated with the Cornish parish of Cury.

CORNELLY
(Pron. "cawr-NELL-ee") The church of this name near Tregony seems to be dedicated to CORNELIUS, Bishop of Rome, who is venerated as a martyr.

COSTENTYN
(Pron. "coss-STENT-in") The Cornish form of CONSTANTINE (Welsh CYSTENNIN), the name of the first Christian emperor. There was also a Cornish St. Constantine who, according to tradition, abandoned his kingdom to become a monk. His name lives on in Constantine (earlier Langostentyn), near Falmouth, and in Constantine Bay near Padstow. In its anglicized form CONSTANTINE the name was not uncommon in Cornwall up to about the middle of the 18th century.

CUBERT
(Pron. "kew-bert") Cubert, near Newquay, is believed to take its name from an obscure Celtic saint whose name may account for the Cardinganshire place-name GWBERT. Some authorities believe that Cubert church is dedicated to the Englishman St. Cuthbert of Lindisfarne. There are records of the use of the saint's name as a Cornish christian name.

CUBY
See KEBY.

DAVETH
The Cornish form of the scriptural name DAVID. Occurs in Cornish literary sources and = the Welsh name DAFYDD.

+DAVY
A pet-form of DAVID not uncommon in pre-18th century Cornwall. The surnames DAVIE and DAV(E)Y are chiefly Cornish and Devonian.

DÉ or DAY
(Pron. "day") A British saint who gave his name to St.Day, near Redruth. Some authorities identify him with the St. Dei venerated in Brittany.

DEGYMAN
(Pron. "de-GIMM-an") St. Degyman (DECUMAN) was venerated at Watchet in Somerset and in South Wales, where the chapel at LLANDDEGYMAN, Breconshire, bore his name. In Cornwall it seems to occur in the place-name DEGIBNA, Helston, allegedly the site of a medieval chapel dedicated in his honour. The name is ultimately from Latin DECUMANUS, "a farmer of tithes".

DEWY
A Cornish form of the scriptural name DAVID found as a Bod. Man. name and as a place-name element; e.g. as the old name for Davidstow, "Dewstow".

+DIGORY
Possibly from the French ÉGARÉ, "strayed", DIGORY seems to go back to the medieval romance of "Sir Degore". Although found elsewhere, DIGORY came to be regarded as mainly Cornish. Obsolete or rare since the end of the last century.

DONYERTH or DONYARTH
A Primitive Cornish name reconstructed from the inscription on the well-known cross base with Hiberno-Saxon interlacings at St. Cleer. The inscription reads: DONIERT ROGAUIT PRO ANIMA, "Doniert ordered this stone for the good of the soul". This Doniert may have been the same person as the semi-historical DUNGARTH, King of Cornwall. Whatever the connection, the approximate pronunciation of the two names would have been "donn-YERTH" and "donn-YARTH". Cf. the Old Welsh name DUNGARTH, from British DUBNOGARTOS.

EDERN
PN A RS Old Cornish name = the Old Welsh name EDEYRN and the Old Breton name EDERN, from Latin AETURNUS.

ELEDER
PN A RS Old Cornish name = the Old Welsh name ELIDIR.

ELWYN
St. Elwyn is said to have been one of a band of Irish saints who landed in Cornwall in the 5th century. A chapel at Sithney records his name and the modern church at Hayle is dedicated in his honour. St. Elwyn's written Life existed at Breage in 1538 but has not survived.

ENODER
An obscure Celtic saint who gave his name to St. Enoder, near Newquay. There are several records of the use of ENODER as a christian name.

ENODOK
(Pron. "enna-DOK") An obscure Celtic saint who gave his name to St. Enodoc, near Padstow. He was honoured during the Middle Ages at Bodmin Priory as St. WENEDOC. The name could be restored as GWENEDOK. See Introduction, page 11.

ENYON
The name of a legendary ruler of Cornwall = the Old Welsh name EINEON, from Late Latin ANNIANUS.

ERBYN
PN An ERBYN was said to have been the father of St. Selevan.

ERVAN
The name-saint of the parish of St. Ervan. Although the present dedication is to St. Hermes, it seems likely that the man behind the name bore a British name like *ERMIN- or *ARMIN-.

EVAL
(Pron. to rhyme with "revel" and not "evil") A saint who is no more than a bare name. It is possible that EVAL is from Latin HUMILIS, from which is derived the Cornish word HUVEL, "humble".

FEOK
(Pron. "fee-OK") St. Feok is assumed to have been a man, but in Latin references of the Middle Ages the name has the feminine form FEOCA. Prof. Loth regarded the name as a corruption of MAEOC. In Finistere St. Maeoc is eponym of the parish of Lanveoc, a name practically identical with the LAFEAGE or LA FEOCK near Feock church. The Cornish surname VAGUE/VAGE, which derives from this parish, preserves the older pronunciation of FEOK, "fay-ok" or "fay-ek". Cf. the name MAYEK/MAYOK.

FRYEK or FRYOK
(Pron. "free-ek"/"free-OK") A RS Bod. Man. name and a place-name

element = the Old Welsh name FRIOC, perhaps from FRI, "nostril".

+GAWEN
(Pron. "gaou-en") One of the most famous of the Arthurian knights, nephew of King Arthur, and probably the original hero of the Grail quest. He appears in the Welsh TRIADS and the MABINOGION as "Gwalchmei". It is believed that GAWEN (Gawain, Gawayne and Gavain are Frenchified spellings) is a genuine Welsh name corresponding to an Old Breton name GAUEN found in UUOI-GAUAN. An alternative suggestion connects the name with the Old German name GAWIN. Fairly popular in Cornwall up to the end of the 17th century.

GENNYS
A little-known Celtic saint whose name is perpetuated in St. Gennys, near Bude.

GERENS
(Pron. "gerr-anz") The Cornish form of the well-known Welsh name GERAINT, from British GERONTIUS. According to legend, St. Gerens, who is patron of Gerrans, was a king of Cornwall. It seems likely that legend had confused him with an authentic early Cornish petty king of the same name. There are many records of the use of the name GERENS as a Cornish christian name.

GERMO(GH)
An obscure, possibly Irish, saint who gave his name to Germoe, near Helston. The name is from Latin GERMOCHUS.

GLEWAS or GLEWYAS
(Pron. to rhyme with the surname "Lewis") A British saint, probably from Wales, who gave his name to St. Gluvias, near Penryn. The name may be a derivative of GLEW, "clear", "bright". The forms GLEWYAS/GLEWYATH of medieval documents survive in the Cornish surname GLUYAS. Cf. the name BUTHEK.

GORGANS
(Pron. "gawr-GANZ") A RS Bod. Man. name and a place-name element = the Old Welsh name GUORCANT, from British VOR-CANTOS, "very white/splendid".

GORHEDER
PN (Pron. "gawr-HEDD-er") A place-name and a RS Bod. Man. name = the Old Welsh name GUORHITIR, from British VOR-SETROS, "very bold".

GORLAS
(Pron. "gawr-luz") The Gorlois of Arthurian legend and a place-name

Ruined Church of St Constantine,
near Trevose Head (see Costentyn).

King Doniert Stone, St Cleer, Near Liskeard
(See Donyerth)

element. GORLAS corresponds to the Old Welsh name GORLOES and the Old Breton name UUORLOIES, and may mean "very pure/holy".

GORNEVES
PN (Pron. "gawr-NEVV-uz") A RS Old Cornish name = the Old Welsh name GURNIVET, from British VOR-NEMETOS, "very holy".

GORON
(Pron. to rhyme with "foreign") A Celtic saint who gave his name to Gorran, near Mevagissey. There is also a St. Guron's well at Bodmin. The name means "hero". Cf. CASWORON.

GORTHELYK
(Pron. "gawr-THEL-ik" with the "th" soft as in "then") A RS Bod. Man. name = the Old Welsh name GURDILIC, "very beloved".

GOURGY
(Pron. "goor-gee") A RS Bod. Man. name and a place-name element. The name means "man dog".

GRYFFYN
This name is found in the Cornwall Domesday and in a late 14th century Cornish literary source. Regarded by christian name investigators as a diminutive or alternative form of GRIFFITH, GRIFFIN occurs in the Middle Ages in counties bordering Wales and has since given rise to an uncommon but fairly widely distributed surname.

GRIFYUTH or GRIFFUTH
(Modern pron. as in the surname "Griffith") A RS Bod. Man. name = the Old Welsh name GRIPHIUD, now spelt GRUFFUDD, and frequently anglicized as GRIFFITH. The second element is IUTH, "lord". Because of the name's Welsh associations, it is perhaps best avoided by those who seek unmistakably Cornish names.

GWALATHER
PN (gwoll-LATH-ur") A RS Old Cornish name = the Old Breton name UUALATR, "leader".

GWENDERN
A RS Bod. Man. name meaning "white/splendid lord". The last element in the name, TEGERNO-, "lord", is also the last element in the Cornish word for "king", "myghtern". Although the church at Wendron is now dedicated to a female WENDRONA, it seems likely that the real name-saint of the parish was one GWENDERN, an otherwise unknown Cornish, Breton or Welsh male missionary. From 1500 to about 1800 the place-name Wendron is often found as Gwendron, its more Cornish form.

GWITHYEN
(Pron. with the "th" soft as in "then") Nothing is known about the saint whose name is perpetuated in Gwithian, near Hayle. A name corresponding to the Old Breton name UUETHIEN seems to occur in at least two Cornish place-names.

GWELESYK
PN (Pron. "go-LEZZ-ik") A RS Old Cornish name = the Old Breton name UUOLETIC, a derivative of GWLAS, "nation".

GWORYEN
PN A RS Old Cornish name = the Old Breton name UUORIEN, from British VOR-GENOS.

GWYDEL
PN (Pron. to rhyme with "fiddle") A RS Old Cornish name = the Old Welsh name GUITAL, from Latin VITALIS.

GWYNHELEK
PN (Pron. "gwinn-HEL-lik") A RS Old Cornish name = the Old Breton name UUINHAELOC, from UUIN, "white/splendid" and HAELOC, a derivative of HAEL, "generous".

GWYNEK or GWYNOK
St. Gwynok, who may have been a Welshman, lived after the "Age of the Saints". About the year 700 he helped to found a monastery in Flanders. In Cornwall his name, which means "little fair one", is associated with the parish of St. Winnow, and is found in several place-names.

GWYNOW
PN (Pron. "gwinn-O") A RS Old Cornish name = the Old Breton name UUINOU, probably a derivative of UUIN, "fair/splendid".

GWYNWALLO(W)
(Pron. "gwinn-WOLL-O") The great British saint who founded the famous monastery of Landevennec in Brittany. Landewednack (earlier Landewenek) is the same name, and nearby Gunwalloe (earlier Gwynwalla) preserves the name of the saint himself. GWYNWALLO(W) = the Old Breton name UUINUUOLOE.

GWYNYER
According to a Life of St. Gwynyer written 800 years after his death, he was the leader of a party of Irish migrants murdered by the pagan King Teudar. He may have been a Welsh missionary. His name apparently = Welsh GUINIER and Breton GUIGNER.

GWYTHENEK
(Pron. "gwa-THEN-ek") The name of a saint honoured in Brittany and Cornwall. There are indications that St. Gwythenek was one of the earlier saints, and that his cult at Padstow and Bodmin diminished following the arrival of St. Petrok. His monastic close, LAN WETHINOC, became the first recorded name for what is now Padstow, and as late as the 16th century the old name survived in the form LODENEK as the true Cornish name for the town. GWYTHENEK is found in at least two place-names and = the Old Breton name UUETHENOC, probably a derivative of UUETH, "battle", "action". As a surname, the saint's name survives to this day in Brittany in the form GUEZENNEC.

GWYTHERYN
PN (Pron. "gwith-THERR-in") A RS Old Cornish name = the Old Welsh name GWYTHERIN.

+HANNIBAL
Phoenician, the name of the great Carthaginian general. Although essentially an Italian name, Hannibal came into use in 16th century Cornwall. Almost exclusively Cornish in distribution ever since. Rare or obsolete for over a century.

+HARVEY
Is probably from HERVE, the French form of Breton HAERVEU, the name of a favourite Breton saint and poet. The name, a compound of Old Breton AER "carnage" and -UIU "worthy", was introduced into England at the time of the Conquest and soon became quite common. It became unfashionable in the 14th century and was in rare use until the 19th century. The name has been included because of its Breton associations.

HEDREK or HEDROK
PN (Pron. "hedd-rek"/"hedd-DROK") A RS Old Cornish name = the Old Breton name HEDROC, a derivative of HEDR, "bold". Possibly the name-saint of Lanhydrock, about whom nothing is known.

HENNA
Apparently a "Cornish" pet-form of HENRY.

HICCA
A "Cornish" pet-form of RICHARD; the equivalent of "Hick" or "Dick".

HORNWALLON
(Pron. "horn-WOLL-un") A RS Old Cornish name from the Bodmin Manumissions, from British ISARNOUALLANOS.

+HOWEL

The Breton name HOEL, corresponding to the Welsh name HYWEL, "eminent", was used from time to time in England during the Middle Ages. Although found as the name of medieval Cornishmen (e.g. Howel de Cruglas, Member of Parliament for Bodmin in 1327), there is no evidence that its use represented the survival of a native Cornish equivalent of HYWEL/HOEL.

+HOCKEN

Hocken, found in early parish registers, is still used as a genuine christian name by at least one Cornish family. It is presumably the obsolete name HALKIN, the diminutive of HAL, a favourite pet-form of HENRY.

JACCA

A "Cornish" equivalent of JACK.

JAGO

A British form of JAMES, from Latin JACOBUS, found as a place-name element and surviving in the modern surname. It corresponds to Welsh IAGO, and like all other Cornish names ending in-O, it has no connection whatever with Spain.

JAMMA

An earlier "Cornish" pet-form of JAMES. Various 17th century sources indicate that JAMES was pronounced JAMMEZ by contemporary Cornishmen.

JEFFRA

A pre-17th century colloquial form of GEOFFREY. Middle English GEFFREY seems to represent two, if not three, Old German names, the second element in all of which is FRITHU, "peace". Cf. Welsh SIEFFRE.

JERMYN or GERMAN

Latin GERMANUS, "a German". Although found outside Cornwall, the name's former popularity among Cornishmen may have owed something to the fact that St. Germanus of Auxerre is patron of St. Germans and Rame.

JORY

Is thought to be a pet-form of GEORGE, for which it is used by modern writers in Cornish.

+JOSE

A common medieval name used for both men and women in the forms JOSSE, GOCE, etc. Along with the O-suffix names it gave further substance to legends about Spanish influence on Cornwall. It has no connection whatever with Spanish JOSE and seems to be the name of a 7th century Breton saint, JODOC, son of JUDICAEL, a hermit of Ponthieu. His cult spread through France and eventually reached Southern Germany. As a man's name JOSE died out in the 14th century; as a woman's name it was virtually obsolete when revived in the 1900's in the form JOYCE. A not uncommon Cornish surname, JOSE seems to be used as second-name by a least two Cornishmen.

JOWAN
The Cornish form of JOHN, like Old Welsh JOUAN, Old Breton IOUUAN, from Latin JOHANNES by way of British. The earlier pronunciation rhymed with the surname "Owen", but by the 17th century the name was pronounced. JOOAN, the spelling used by the Cornish writer Nicholas Boson.

KÉ, KEA or KAY
(Pron. "kay") A British saint who gave his name to Kea, near Truro. According to Breton legend, St. Ké founded a monastery at Cleder and later returned to Britain to try and make peace between King Arthur and Modred. The name is said to be from Latin CAIUS.

KEBY or CUBY
(Pron. "kebb-ee"/"kew-bee") According to tradition, St. Keby was actually Cornish-born, the son of St. Selevan. He is patron of Duloe and Tregony. Early spellings of his name, allied to evidence from Wales, show that CUBY is corrupt.

KENAL
PN (Pron. to rhyme with "kennel") A RS Old Cornish name = the Old Welsh name CYNHAEL, from the British CUNOSAGLOS, "generous chief". KENNAL is found twice as an early 16th century christian name, but seems likely to be for the surname KENALL.

KENAN
PN A form of CONAN resulting from vowel reduction. See CONAN.

KENBRES
PN (Pron. "kenn-brez") A RS Old Cornish name = the Old Breton name CONBRIT and the Old Welsh name CYNBRYD.

KENEDER
PN (Pron. "ke-NEDD-ur") A RS Old Cornish name = the Old Welsh name CYNIDR, from British CUNO-SETROS, "bold chief".

KENDERN
PN A RS Old Cornish name = the Old Welsh name CYNDEYRN, from British CUNO-TIGERNOS, "chief lord".

KENGAR

St. Kengar was venerated in Wales and Brittany and a chapel at Lanivet bore his name. The unreduced form of the name is almost certainly evident in the place-name TREGONGER and = the Old Breton name CONGAR.

KENHEBRES

PN (Pron. "kenn-HEBB-riz") A RS Old Cornish name = the Old Welsh name CONHIBRIT.

KENHORN

PN A RS Old Cornish name = the Old Welsh name CYNHAERN, from CUNO-ISARNOS, "iron chief". Occurs in the place-name Linkinhorne (LAN KENHORN), "monastic enclosure (of) Kenhorn", and is the last element in the well-known Cornish surname POLKINHORN.

KENOW

PN (Pron. "kenn-o") A RS Old Cornish name = the Old Welsh name CENAU and the Old Breton name CANAO, from British CONOUIOS. Its literal meaning seems to be "cub".

KENVER

PN A RS Old Cornish name = the Old Welsh name CYNFOR, probably from British CUNO-MORUS, "great chief". According to the 19th century Life of St. Paul Aurelian, King Mark of Cornwall was also known by the name of CONOMOR.

KENWAL

PN (Pron. "kenn-woll") A RS Old Cornish name = the Old Welsh name CYNWAL, from British CUNO-UALLOS, "powerful chief". Cognate with the Irish name CONALL.

KENWYN

PN A RS Old Cornish name = the Old Welsh name CENWYN, from British CUNO-UINDOS, "white/splendid chief". Possibly the name-saint of Kenwyn, Truro, though early spellings of this place-name suggest that it may mean "while ridge".

KENWYTHEN

PN (Pron. "kenn- WITH-en") A RS Old Cornish name = the Old Welsh name CONGUETHEN and the Old Breton name KENGUETHEN, from CUNO-, "high/lofty" and a derivative of UUETH, "battle".

KEVERN

Nothing is known about the saint who gave his name to St. Kevern. His name appears to be a corruption of some name like AKEVRAN. It has been suggested that it is Irish AED COBHRAN. KEVERN has been used as a christian name.

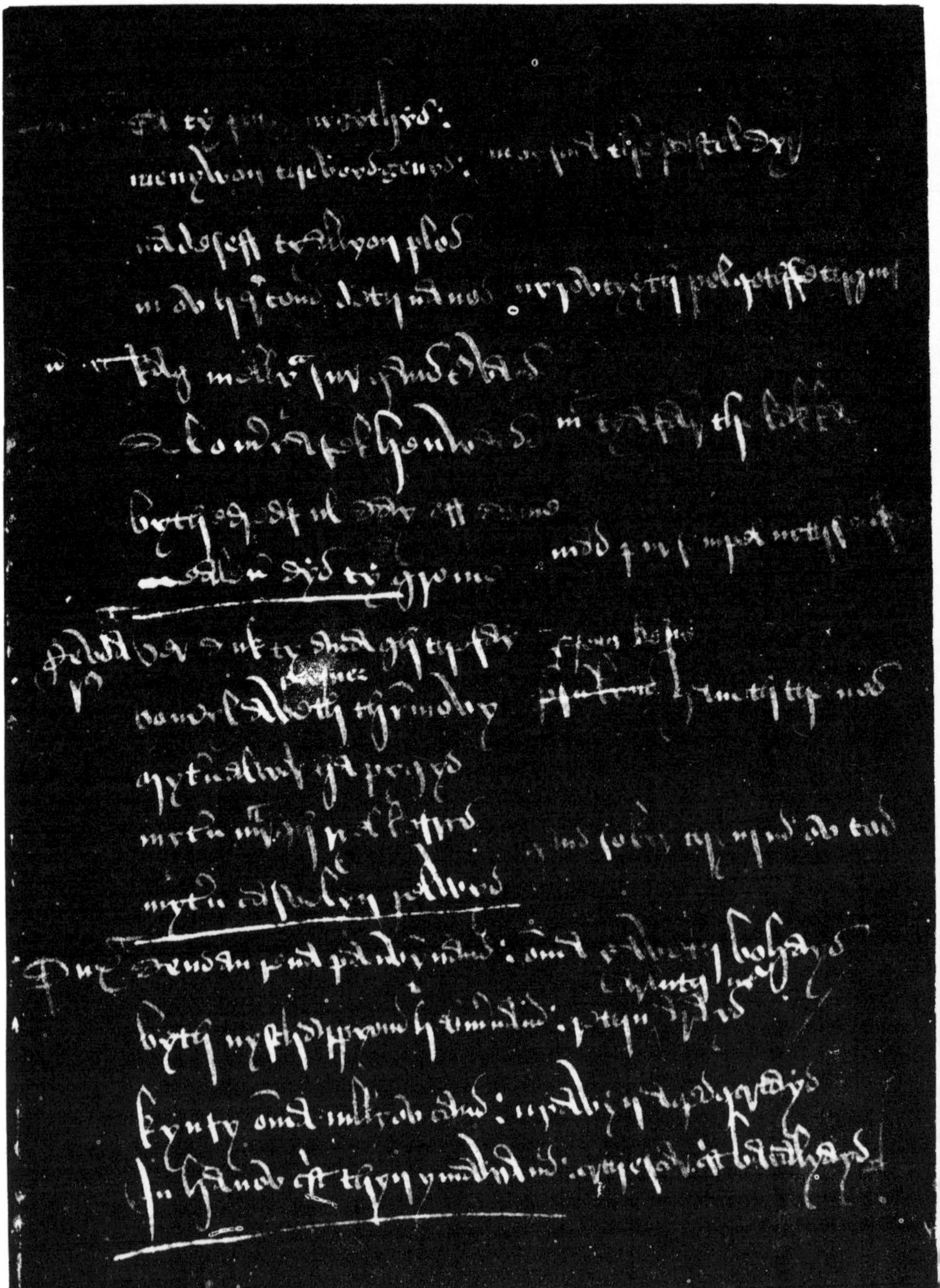

KITTO(W)
A Cornish O-suffix pet-form of CHRISTOPHER.

LALLOW
Found as the christian name of at least two early 16th century Cornishmen. Menheniot church is dedicated to St. Lalluwy, whose name-according to Charles Henderson - is found corrupted to LALLOW in 1500.

LEW
PN A RS Old Cornish name = the Old Welsh name LLEU, "guide", "ruler".

LEWYTH
PN A RS Old Cornish name = the Old Welsh name LLYWEITH, "ruler". Found inscribed on a Camborne altar-stone and recorded as a Cornish word in a 12th century glossary of Cornish words.

LOCRYN
A not uncommon christian name in pre-18th century Cornwall.

LOWTHAS
PN (Pron. with the "th" soft as in "then") A RS Old Cornish name = the Old Welsh name LLEUDDAD.

LUK
(Pronounced "leek") The Middle Cornish form of the name LUKE.

LYWARGH
PN (Pron. "loo-arh") A RS Old Cornish name = the Old Welsh name LLYWARCH.

MABAN
PN An Old Cornish name = the Old Breton name MABAN, possibly a derivative of MAB, "son".

MADERN
A saint, probably Welsh, who gave his name to Madron, near Penzance. The not uncommon surname MADDERN preserves the older form of the name. Cf. the surnames GLUYAS and BIDDICK.

MALSCOS
PN A RS Old Cornish name = the Old Breton name MAELSCUET, from MAEL, "prince", and SCUET "shield". The surname TREVASKIS contains this name.

+MANUEL and EMANUEL
Hebrew, "God with us". Although essentially a Spanish and Portuguese name, EMANUEL and its shortened form MANUEL enjoyed

considerable popularity in pre-18th century Cornwall.

MARGH
(Pron. "marh") The Cornish form of MARK, by way of British from Latin MARCUS. Found in the play "Bewnans Meryasek" and as a place-name element.

MASEK or MADOK
PN (Pron. "mazz-ek"/"mad-DOK") A RS Old Cornish name corresponding to the Welsh name MADOG, which has long been a favourite Welsh christian name. There is much to be said for preferring the Middle Cornish place-name form of the name, MASEK, which is unlikely to be mistaken for the Welsh name.

MASSEN
The name of a traditional Cornish king in the play "Bewnans Meryasek". It has been suggested that the occurrence of his name may indicate that in late 15th century Cornwall there was still a lingering tradition of Maximus, the Macsen Wledig of Wales.

MAWGAN
A British saint who gave his name to St. Mawgan-in-Pyder and to Mawgan-in-Meneage. The name is from British MAGLOCUNOS, "lofty/mighty prince". Although MALGAN would be more correct, it was as MAWGAN that 17th century Cornishmen bore the name.

MAYEK or MAYOK
PN Prof. Loth believed that the name FEOK is a corruption of MAYOK. MAYOK, from British MAGIACOS, corresponds to the Old Breton name MAIOC and seems to occur in at least one place-name. See FEOK.

MELOR
A Breton saint who is patron of Mylor and Linkinhorne.

MERYASEK
(Pronounced "murr-YAZZ-ek") St. Meryasek is the subject of the play in Cornish, BEWNANS MERYASEK, "Life of Meryasek". Although patron of Camborne, St. Meryasek is now perhaps best known in Brittany, where his name takes the form MERIADEK.

MERYN
PN A RS Old Cornish name = the Old Welsh name MERIN and the Old Breton name MEREN. It seems likely that the church at St. Merryn was originally dedicated to a male missionary who bore this name, and that it was later re-dedicated to St. Marina.

MERYEN
PN (Pron. to rhyme with "Veryan") A RS Old Cornish name = the Old Welsh name MERIAWN and the Old Breton name MERION, from Late Latin MARIANUS.

MEWAN
A saint, according to tradition a Welshman, who gave his name to St. Mewan. Cf. the Breton saint's name MEVEN.

MODRED
The Modred of Arthurian romance. In Cornwall the name is found as a Bodmin Manumissions name and as a place-name element, e.g. in CARVEDDRAS (KAER VODRES, 1342). The name has been left in its Old Cornish form.

MYGHAL
(Pron. "ma-HAIL") A Middle Cornish form of MICHAEL found in Middle Cornish literature. Occurs as MEHALE, etc., in at least two late place-names.

MILYAN
The name of a legendary ruler of Cornwall and also a Bod. Man. name. The name-saints of Mullion and of St. Mellion may have borne this name, which is apparently from Late Latin AEMILIANUS.

MILYEK or MILYOK
PN A RS Old Cornish name, probably from Latin AEMILIACUS.

NADELEK
(Pron. "no-DELL-ek") Cornish, "Christmas Day". Occurs in the extinct Cornish surname NADELACK, which suggests that the name may have been used as a Cornish equivalent of NOEL.

NERTH
D Cornish, "strength". May occur as a nickname in the place-name TRENARTH.

NEYTHEN
PN (Pron. "nigh-thun") The Cornish form of the Irish name NECTAN, which, as the name of a saint, is perpetuated in St. Nectan, near Lostwithiel. The name seems to occur in several place-names, but is possibly for EYTHYN, "furze-bush", in some cases.

NICCA
Apparently a "Cornish" pet-form of NICHOLAS.

OMFFRA or OMFRA
A pre-16th century colloquial form of HUMPHREY. Old English HUNFRITH,

31

HUNFRITH, a compound of the folk-name HUNI and FRITH "peace", was reinforced by Norman ONFROI (from the cognate Old German HUNFRID), which became UMFRAY, HUMFREY or HUMFRYE in English use. In Cornish use Norman-introduced names ending in -FROI, from FRITHU "peace", are sometimes found with the ending -FRA long after -FRY, -FREY or -FRAY had become usual in their English counterparts. Cf. JEFFRA, REMFRA, an early variant of REMFRY, and the Welsh form of Humphrey, WMFFRE.

+OTES
Old German AUDO, later ODO or OTHO, a derivative of AUDA "rich". ODO and OTHO crossed the Channel with the Normans and are found as OTES in later medieval England. In Cornwall OTES and OTTY are found up to the early part of the 17th century.

PADERN
According to tradition, St. Padern was a Cornish chieftain and father of St. Costentyn. He is patron of North and South Petherwin. The name is from Latin PATERNUS.

PASCO(W)
The accepted view is that the name is from Cornish PASK, "Easter", with a Cornish -O/-OW suffix meaning "of". If this is correct, PASCOW is the Cornish counterpart of the obsolete English name PASCAL and of the surviving Breton name PASCOU. An alternative suggestion, based on the theory that the -O/-OW suffix had a diminutive function, is that PASCOW is a diminutive of the obsolete English name PASK, which had the same meaning as the Cornish word. PASCOW was a fairly common name for Cornish boys until the first few decades of the 18th century.

PAWLY
A fairly common 17th century form of PAUL.

PAWLYN
PN A RS Old Cornish name from Latin PAULINUS.

PEDER
(Pron. "pay-dur") The Cornish form of PETER. The spelling PEDYR is encountered as frequently as the spelling PEDER.

PENCAST
Cornish, "Whitsuntide", "Pentecost". The Christian name PENTECOST, from the Gweek word for Whitsuntide, was in general use until the 17th century, when it became rare and increasingly associated with Cornwall, where it survived until the end of the last century. The Cornish name for Whitsuntide is found as a surname (e.g. Saundry Pencaste, St. Ives, 1605) and may have been used as a christian name.

PEDREK or PETHEREK

Petherick and Peddrick are recorded as Cornish christian names up to the first quarter of the 18th century and seem to preserve the otherwise unrecorded Middle Cornish form of Petrok, *PEDREK. Cf. 14th century forms of the place-name Trebetherick.

PERAN or PERRAN

The saint who gave his name to Perranzabuloe, Perranporth, Perranarworthal and Perranuthnoe. Patron of Cornish miners and acclaimed by many as Patron Saint of Cornwall. As a christian name PER(R)AN seems to have survived until the beginning of the 19th century. The spelling PIRAN, leading inevitably to the pronunciation "pie-ran", is incorrect and is based on the erroneous identification of St. Per(r) an with a quite different saint.

PETROK

St. Petrok vies with St. Peran for the title of Patron Saint of Cornwall. Probably from South Wales, he settled at what is now Padstow (Petrok's stow). His name, which corresponds to the Welsh name PEDROG, was used as a christian name by pre-18th century Cornishman. The form PEDROK would be nearer the sound of his name in Old Cornish, but PETRO(C)K seems to be too well established to tamper with.

RAW

A colloquial form of RALPH current in pre-18th century Cornwall. Ralph, from Old English RAEDWULF (=Old Norse RATHULFR), a compound of RAED "counsel" and WULF "wolf", was later reinforced by Norman influence. It developed into RAUF or RAFF, which were the usual forms of the name until the 17th century. Carew (1555-1620) regarded RAW as the Cornish counterpart of RAFE, the standard form of the name by his time.

+RAWLYN

A diminutive of RAOUL, the French form of RADULF. Not uncommon outside Cornwall in the Middle Ages. Survived in Cornish use until the latter part of the 16th century if not later.

REMFRY

Old German RAGANFRID, a compound of RAGAN "might" and FRITHU "peace" RENFRED crossed the Channel with the Normans and was fairly common elsewhere up to the 16th century. In its usual Cornish form, REMFRY, the name became obsolete in the last century, but as RENFRED it still survives as Cornish christian name.

+ RENOWDEN
Old English REGENWEALD, a compound of REGEN and WEALD, both of which mean "power", "force". After the Conquest the name was reinforced by Norman REYNAUD, of which RENOWDEN is a diminutive. The name still survived in Cornwall at the beginning of the 18th century.

REWAN (RUMON)
St. Rewan/Rumon gives his name to Ruan Lanihorne and to other places in Cornwall and Devonshire. The discrepancy between REWAN (or RUAN if preferred) and RUMON is explained by the fact that Old Cornish had a weakly nasal "v" which sounded something like an "m". Since there was no letter in the Latin alphabet to represent "v", "m" was used in its place. Such a "v" occurs in Rumon, which is essentially a literary or anglicized form; Rewan, on the other hand, preserves the later colloquial (and more correct) form of the name. The name also occurs in the Bod. Man.

RYEL or RYOL
(Pron. "ree-el"/"ree-ol") Found as a Bod. Man. name, as the name of a traditional Cornish king in the play "Bewnans Meryasek", and as a possible place-name element. Possibly from British RIGALIS.

SADORN
PN A RS Old Cornish name, from Latin SATURNUS, "Saturn". The word for "Saturday" in Cornish.

SALAN
An Old Cornish name found in the Bod. Man. and probably in the place-name CARSELLA (KARSALAN, 1086).

+SAMSON
Hebrew, "child of Shamash (the sun-god)". The name of the champion of the Israelites and of a Welsh bishop who passed through Cornwall on his way to Brittany. He is patron of Golant and gave his name to one of the Isles of Scilly. Once fairly common everywhere, SAMSON became virtually obsolete after the Reformation. Still survives in Cornwall.

SEBASTIAN
See BASTIAN

SANTO
A Cornish O-suffix pet-form of ALEXANDER.

SELEVAN
(Pron. "se-LEV-vun") The Cornish form of SOLOMON. St. Selevan gave his name to St. Levan and is said to have been the father of St. Keby.

34

SILYEN (Properly SULYEN)

The original patron of Luxulyan. SILYEN = the Old Welsh name SELIEN and the Old Breton name SULENN, from SULGENOS, "sun born".

SITHNY

The saint who gave his name to Sithney is the same person as the Breton St. Sezni.

TALAN

An Old Cornish name found in the Bod. Man. and as a place-name element. TALAN = the Old Breton name TALAN and is a derivative of TAL, "forehead". Possibly the unknown name-saint of Talland.

TALEK

A Cornish adjective meaning "big-browed" which may account for the surname TALLACK. A suitable first-name.

TANGY or TANGUY

(Pron. "tann-gee") This Breton christian name was introduced into England by Breton followers of the Conqueror, and is especially common as a surname in eastern England. Cornish bearers of the surname may be descended from the Breton labourers, artisans and curates who settled in medieval Cornwall. The name is still fairly common in Brittany as a christian name and means "fire dog".

TEUDAR or TEWDAR

The pagan tyrant in the Cornish play "Bewnans Meryasek" and the traditional enemy of the early Christian missionaries in Cornwall. His name (or that of another Teudar) survives in the St. Kevern place-name LESTOWDER, "court(of) Teudar".

TRYSTAN or TRISTAN

The hero of medieval romance, newphew of King Mark of Cornwall, lover of Eseld. The name is thought to derive from DRUSTAN, a known British name which later became influenced by French TRISTE, "sad". TRISTAN seems to occur in the place-name TREDRESTAN and may be preserved, in its older form, in the inscription on the famous inscribed stone at Menabilly. TRISTRAM, TRUSTRAM and TRISTRAN are medieval English perversions of the name and are not suitable for Cornish use.

TUDWAL

PN A RS Old Cornish name = the Middle Welsh name TUDWAL, from British TOTO-UALOS, "people powerful".

TUDY
(Pron. "tew-dee") A little-known saint who gave his name to the parish of St. Tudy.

UDY
(Pron. "ew-dee") Not uncommon as a 16th century Cornish christian name.

UNY or EWNY
An obscure Celtic saint who is patron of Redruth and Lelant, and joint patron of Crowan. His name has been used as a christian name.

UST
(Pron. "east") Very little is known about the saint who gave his name to St. Just-in-Roseland and to St. Just-in-Penwith. In Cornish mouths his name, from Latin JUSTUS, was pronounced "east".

UTHER
Occurs in 16th and 17th century parish registers. A legendary king of the Britons; by an adulterous association with Y-gerna, wife of Gorlois, Duke of Cornwall, he became the father of Arthur, who succeeded him.

WELLA
A "Cornish" pet-form of WILLIAM. Regarded by at least two 17th century Cornishmen as the Cornish equivalent of the name.

YESTIN
A Yestin was said to be a son of St. Gerens. The name occurs in the Bod. Man. and, like Welsh IESTIN and English JUSTIN, is said to be a derivative of Latin JUSTUS.

YLLOGAN or ILLOGAN
A saint who gave his name to Illogan. Cf. the Old Breton name ILLOC, of which ILLOGAN may be a derivative.

YTHEL or possibly YETHEL
It is believed that Cornish bearers of the surname JEWELL perpetuate the name IUDHAEL, "generous lord", which is thought to have been reintroduced by early Breton settlers. The name seems to occur in the Cornish place-name TRETHILL (TREYUTHEL 1393, 1394). The suggested modern form YTHEL takes into account the later development of the language and corresponds to the modern Welsh name ITHEL.

YTHGANS
PN A RS Old Cornish name = the Old Breton name IUDCANT, "white/splendid lord".

YTHNO(W) or UTHNO(W)
The unknown missionary whose name is coupled with that of St. Peran in
the place-name PERRANUTHNO. The name means "famous lord", from
IUD, "lord", and a suffix meaning "familiar".

NAMES FOR GIRLS

Nearly all of the newly-devised compound names included are based on
names current in Wales, but are sufficiently dissimilar in form not to be
mistaken for Welsh names. They are described as "Cornish compound" to
distinguish them from names made from a single dictionary word. Like
them, they are indicated by a capital "D".

+ANGELET
Angelet is a French feminine diminutive form of the obsolete name
ANGEL, which still survives in Italy as ANGELO. From the Greek word
for "messenger". Found in 17th century Cornish parish registers.

ARGHANS or ARRANZ
D Cornish, "silver". In 17th century Cornwall ARGENTINE was
sometimes used as a christian name.

+ARMYNEL
Armynel was a popular name in 17th century Cornwall. It may be a
diminutive of ARMINE, the English form of French ARMAND.

ATHWENNA
Athwenna is the latinized form of ADWYN, the name of the missionary
remembered at Advent, near Camelford. She is said to have been one of the
daughters of the semi-historical King Brychan of Wales.

BANALLEN
D (Pron. "ba-NALL-en") Cornish, "broom flower".

BARENWYN
D (Pron. "ba-REN-win") Cornish compound meaning "fair branch".

+BEATEN
Latin, "bringer of joy". A common medieval diminutive form of
BEATRIX. Still survived in 17th century Cornwall.

BENNATH
D Cornish, "a blessing".

BERLEWEN
D (Pron. "bur-LEW-en") Cornish, "Venus", "morning star".

37

+BERSABA
A medieval form of BATHSHEBA which still survived in early 18th century Cornwall.

BERYAN
The name-saint of St. Buryan.

BLEJAN
D Cornish, "bloom".

BLEJENNYK
D (Pron. "bla-JENN-ik") Cornish, "little bloom".

BLEJWYN
D Cornish compound meaning "fair flower", the Cornish equivalent of Welsh BLODWEN.

BORA or BORRA
D Cornish, "dawn".

BRONNEN
D Cornish, "a rush".

BRYLUEN
D Cornish, "rose".

CAJA
D Cornish, "daisy".

+CHESTEN
Old English CHRISTEN, "Christian". A form of CHRISTINE in use in 17th century Cornwall.

COLUMBA
A feminine form of COLUM given to 17th century St. Columb girls.

CONWENNA
A name from legend. Conwenna was the daughter of a legendary ruler of Cornwall.

+CORDELIA
When used today it is probably always taken from Shakespeare's KING LEAR. The name may be the same as CORDULA, which appears in Welsh and Cornish calendars as the name of one of the companions of St. Ursula. Since CORDELIA occurs quite frequently in early Cornish parish registers, it may have been a traditional name in Cornwall.

CREWENNA
The latinized form of the name of the saint remembered at Crowan.

38

The Tristan Stone, Menabilly, Near Fowey.

10th century stone carving of
St Petroc, in Padstow Parish
Church.

Cross of St Peran, Perranporth, mentioned
in a charter of 960 A.D.

39

CRYDA or CREEDA
(Pron. "creed-a") The patron of Creed, near Grampound. Nothing is known about her.

DELEN or DELLEN
D Cornish, "petal".

DELENNYK
D Cornish, "little petal".

DEMELZA
A place-name in the parish of St. Wenn. DEMELZA has been used in recent years as a pleasant-sounding girls' name. For those who are more concerned with euphony than meaning (DEMELZA may mean "hill-fort of Maeldaf") there are many other place-names which can be used as names for girls. E.g. LAMORNA, MORVA, LAMANVA. CLODAGH, the name of a river in Tipperary, is only one example of the scores of place-names and river names which have been used as christian names.

DEROWEN
D (Pon. "der-ROW-en") Cornish, "oak".

DERWA
Late medieval sources link St. Derwa with St. Ya. Her name is perpetuated in Menedarva, Camborne, formerly MERTHER DERWA, "chapel (of) Derwa".

+DONAT or DONNET
Latin, "given". Given to boys as well as girls in the Middle Ages, DONAT remained in Cornish use as a name for girls until as late as 1755.

DYWANA
The name of a legendary ruler of Cornwall.

EBREL
D Cornish, "April".

ELESTREN
D (Pron. "el-LEST-ren") Cornish, "iris".

ELOWEN
D (Pron. el-LOW-en") Cornish, "elm".

+EMBLYN
Properly EMMELINE, from Old French AMELINE. A common name in the Middle Ages. In the form EMBLYN it is still found in late 17th century Cornish parish registers.

ENDELYON
Patron of Endellion, near Port Isaac.

ENOR
D Cornish, "honour"

EPPOW
Occurs in the 16th century as a rare name for West Cornish girls. R. Morton Nance suggested that EPPOW is a Cornish O-suffix pet-form of ELIZABETH. If so, EPPOW would have been formed from IBBET, the usual diminutive of ISABEL (LA), the French and Spanish form of ELIZABETH and one of the commonest female names in the 13th and 14th centuries. Cf. RICHOW.

ESYLD or ESELD
The heroine of the Tristan romances, wife of King Mark of Cornwall and lover of Tristan. Unfortunately, the Old Cornish form of the name has not survived in Cornish use. There can be little doubt that it occurs in HRYT ESELT, "Eselt's ford", a lost St. Keverne place-name mentioned in a charter of 967. This Old Cornish name corresponds to the Middle Welsh name ESYLLT, and would have become *ESELS or *EJELS in later Cornish use. ESELT/ESYLLT may possibly derive from a British *ADSILTIA and mean something like "she who is gazed at". It was a common name in the Middle Ages, owing its popularity to that of the Tristan romances. It is usually recorded in the latinized form ISOLDA, but the spoken form of the name was derived from French ISEUT, which gave rise to spellings like ISAT and ISSOT. In this form, the name was quite common in pre-17th century Cornwall. Modern parents who wish to use the nme because of its Cornish associations will no doubt prefer to avoid latinized ISOLDA and Frenchified ISEULT. The forms ESYLD and ESELD, based on Old Cornish ESELT, are distinguishingly Cornish and are matched by modern Breton ISILD and modern Welsh ESSYLLT. The pronunciation of the names ESYLD/ESELD is "ez-ZILD"/"ez-ZELD".

+EULALIA
Greek, "sweetly-speaking". Fairly common in France and Spain. EULALIA early names a Cornishwoman when found in Britain. Now obsolete or very rare.

EVA
(Pron. "ayv-a") The Cornish form of EVE.

EWA
Although St. Ewe has been regarded as a woman since at least the 12th century, it is possible that "she" is to be identified with the Breton male saint, St. Eo. The barton adjoining the church of St. Ewe, LANEWA, "monastic close (of) Ewa", preserves an older form of the name.

41

Kenwyn Church, Truro

OPPOSITE Page 95 of BEWNANS MERYASEK, "Life of Meryasek", a long play in Cornish about the life of Meryasek, the son of a Duke of Brittany. Interwoven with it is the legend of St. Sylvester the Pope and the Emperor Constantine. Much of the play's interest derives from the fact that it is set against a Cornish and Breton background and does not follow conventional scriptural lines. The play contains several references to Camborne of which Meryasek was patron, and may have been written for performance over a period of two days at Camborne Feast. The manuscript, which is preserved in the National Library of Wales at Aberystwyth (Peniarth MSS. 105), was written in 1504 by Radulphus Ton, priest, but it is not clear whether he was the author or merely a transcriber. Page 95 has been selected because it contains the names of certain traditional Cornish kings. With the exception of PYGYS, which may have been written for TYGYS or some other name, all have been included in this booklet. The lines containing the names of the kings occur about halfway down the opposite page. They read:-

Ser duk ty a nagh the fay	Sir Duke, thou shalt deny thy faith,
bo neyl presner thymmovy	Or else a prisoner of mine
eseth kens haneth the nos	Thou shalt be before this very night.
mytern alwar ha pygys	King Alwar and Pygys,
mytern margh ryel kefrys	King Margh, Ryel, also
mytern casvelyn gelwys	The king called Casvelyn
gans sokyr thym us ov tos.	With succour are coming to me.

The commoner scriptural names like JOHN occur in their Cornish forms throughout the range of Cornish literature, which comprises the trilogy ORIGO MUNDI, PASSIO DOMINI and RESURRECTIO DOMINI known collectively as the ORDINALIA and probably written in the last quarter of the 14th century; a 259-verse Passion Poem of perhaps the same period; the BEWNANS MERYASEK, and a play known as the GWYRANS AN BYS, "The Creation of the World", transcribed in 1611 but probably composed at least seventy years earlier. A Cornish translation of Bishop Bonner's "Profitable and Necessary Doctrine", providing the longest run of extant Cornish prose, was completed by John Tregear probably between 1555 and 1558. Late Cornish literature (from about 1600 onwards) is on a reduced scale and includes, among other things, a folk tale, an essay on the decline of Cornish, songs, poems, epigrams and mottoes.

FYNA or FEENA
D Cornish, "finer".

GLANDER
D Cornish, "purity".

GLANNA
D Cornish, "purer".

GONNETTA
Gonnetta is found as a 14th century name for Cornish girls. Of uncertain etymology, it may have been formed from the name of the patron of Roche.

GWAYNTEN
D Cornish, "spring".

GWENIVER
An older, more Cornish form of JENIFER found in some early parish registers. See JENIFER.

GWENEP
The name-saint of Gwennap.

GWENNOL
D Cornish, "a swallow".

GWIRYON
D Cornish, "innocent", "sincere".

GWYNDER
D Cornish, "brightness".

HEBASCA
D Cornish, "solace".

HEDRA
D Cornish, "October".

+JAQUET
French feminine diminutive of JACQUES (JAMES). Occurs in Britain from the 13th to 17th centuries. Not uncommon in 17th century Cornwall.

JENIFER
The Welsh name GWENHWYFAR, the name of King Arthur's wife, is believed to account for Anglo-Norman GUENIEVRE, which became GAYNORE or GWENORE in the later English romances. In the forms GUENER and GUEANOR it survived in Lancashire until the beginning of the 17th century. Most authorities believe that the name entered

Cornwall as Anglo-Norman GUENIEVRE, but there are others who maintain that the name may have enjoyed a continuous and independent existence in Cornwall from the earliest times, and that its survival in the heartland of Arthurian tradition owes nothing to the Anglo-Normans. JENIFER (found as GWENIVER in some early parish registers) became appreciably commoner in some parishes in the 18th century, at the very time so many old favourites were disappearing, and is Cornwall's only native name to achieve popularity in Britain as a whole. It is now so common that most people have ceased to regard it as a Cornish name. Cornish tradition seems to uphold the spelling JENIFER.

JENIFRY
Seems to be a Cornish form of WINIFRED. ST. GWENFREWI was said to have been a Welsh princess martyred by Caradoc. The latinized form of her name, WENEFREDA, was anglicized as WINIFRED, and was sometimes confused with the Old English masculine name WINFRITH. That JENIFRY is not a corruption of JENIFER is apparent from the occurance of the name in the form JENEFRED. JENIFRY is presumably from a earlier Anglo-Norman GUENIFROI. Cf. JENIFER and REMFRY.

JENNA, JEDNA and JANA
Seem to be pre-17th century West Cornish forms of JANE, from Old French JEHANE. All three forms seem to have been influenced by the West Cornish linguistic background and may be comparable with other Cornish A-suffix names like WELLA and HICCA.

JOWANET
A diminutive of JOAN (earlier JOHAN), the usual feminine form of JOHN. Fairly common in the earlier West Cornwall parish registers. In the Cornish-speaking area of Cornwall, JOWANET seems likely to have been regarded as an appropriate feminine equivalent of JOWAN, the Cornish form of JOHN. Spellings like GEWANATT and JEWANATT, which follow the Late Cornish pronunciation of JOHN, seem to support this suggestion.

JOWNA
A pre-17th century colloquial form of JO(H)ANNA or possibly a cornicized form of JOHAN, the earlier form of JOAN. Cf. JENNA.

KAYNA, KEYNA or KEYN
St. Keyn, or to give her one of the latinized forms of her name, KAYNA, is the patron of St. Keyne and is one of the better known Cornish saints, owing much of her fame to Southey's humorous poem "The Well of St. Keyne". She is said to have been one of the Children of Brychan. Her name may be derived from Welsh CAIN, "beautiful".

KEKEZZA (Properly KYKESOW)
D Cornish "heath". The best Cornish equivalent of the name "Heather".

KELYNEN
D (Pron. "ke-LINN-en") Cornish, "holly".

KENSA
D Cornish, "first".

KERENSA or KERENZA
(Pron. "ke-RENZ-a") Cornish, "affection", "love". The name is already in use.

KERESEN or KEREZEN
D (Pron. "ke-REZZ-en") Cornish, "cherry".

KERESYK or KEREZIK
D (Pron. "ke-REZZ-ik") Cornish, "dear".

KERRA
D Cornish, "dearer".

KEWA or KEW
Nothing is known about the name-saint of St. Kew, near Wadebridge, except that she was reputed to be the sister of DOCCO, the name of a Glamorgan saint.

KEWERA or KEWERAZ
D (Pron. "ke-WERR-az") Cornish, "fulfilment", "perfection".

LASEK or LADOK
(Pron. "lazz-ek"/"ladd-OK") Practically nothing is known about the saint who gave her name to Ladock. (This place-name made the transition from LADOC to LASEK but has since reverted to LADOCK).

LOVEDAY or LOWDY
A common medieval christian name which has now become confined to Cornwall, where it still survives in occasional use. The name was originally bestowed on boys or girls on a LOVEDAY, a day appointed for a meeting between enemies and litigants with a view to an amicable settlement. Now given only to girls, the name takes the colloquial form LOWDY in some earlier parish registers.

LOWENA or LOWENNA
(Pron. "lo-WENN-a") Cornish, "joy". Already in use as a name.

LOWENEK
D (Pron. "lo-WENN-ek") Cornish, "joyful".

MABENA
(Pron. "ma-been-a") The latinized form of MABYN. Although the patron of St. Mabyn, near Wadebridge, is traditionally a woman, and was depicted as such in the old St. Neot church windows, it seems possible that she may have been a man with a name corresponding to the Old Welsh name MABAN.

+MARIOT
Hebrew, probably, "wished-for-child". The usual diminutive form of MARY in the Middle Ages. Survived in Cornwall as late as 1725.

MARYA
(Pron. "ma-REE-a", like Italian MARIA) The Cornish form of MARY. The late 17th century Cornish writer William Rowe used the spelling MAREEA.

MELDER
D Cornish, "honey-sweetness".

+MELLONEY or MELANIE
Greek, "black". As MELANIA, borne by two Roman saints. MELANIE is popular in France and probably crossed the Channel with Hugenot refugees. Recorded in Cornwall and Devonshire from the 17th century, MELANIE is still in use in Cornwall, where the traditional spelling of the name is MELLONEY. Although regarded as primarily Cornish on this side of the Channel, it is probably no longer possible to separate Cornish tradition from modern French influence.

MELWYN
D A Cornish compound meaning "honey-fair".

MELYONEN
D (Pron. "mell-YONN-en") Cornish, "violet".

MELYOR or MELIORA
Exclusively Cornish in distribution and possible a corruption of a native Celtic name, MELIORA is first recorded in 1218. Very common as MELYOR/MELLEAR in 17th and early 18th century parish registers, the name survived for a while in the last century, generally in the form MELIORA.

MERAUD or MEROUDA
This Cornish name is usually taken to be a contraction of Middle English EMERAUD, "emerald", but is recorded as MEROUDA as early as 1296, which is earlier than the first recorded occurrence of EMERAUD. It has been suggested that MERAUD is a native Cornish name, possibly a derivative of MOR, "sea".

METHEVEN
D (Pron. "me-THEVV-en") Cornish, "June".

MORGELYN
D Cornish, "sea-holly".

MORENWYN
D (Pron. "mor-RENN-win") A Cornish compound meaning "fair maiden".

MORVOREN
D (Pron. "mor-VORR-en") Cornish, "maid of the sea", "mermaid".

MORWENNA
The name-saint of Morwenstow (Morwenna's stow). MORWENNA is already in use.

MORWENNOL
D Cornish, "a sea-swallow", "tern". (The sea-bird).

NESSA
D Cornish, "second" or "nearest".

NEWLYNA
(Pron. "new-LEEN-a") The latinized form of the name of the saint who is remembered at Newlyn, near Newquay.

NONNA or NON
Patron of Altarnon and Pelynt. Very little is known about the real St. Nonna.

PASCA, PASCATTE, PASCES, PASCOWES
Are all feminine forms of the once-common Cornish masculine christian name PASCOW, which derives from Cornish PASK, "Easter".

PESWERA or PEZWERA
D (Pron. "pez-WERR-a") Cornish, "fourth".

+REDIGAN
A fairly common pre-18th century name for Cornish girls. It seems (for an alternative etymology has been suggested) to be the feminine name RADEGUND, from the Old German RADAGUNDIS, a compound of RADI "counsel" and GUNDI "war".

RICHOW
A fairly common pre-17th century name for Cornish girls. The name does not seem to occur in standard reference books; it is perhaps a feminine pet-form of RICHARD, with a Cornish -OW suffix used in a diminutive capacity.

ROSEN or ROZEN
D (Pron. "rozz-en") Cornish "rose".

ROSENWYN
D (Pron. "roz-ZENN-win") A Cornish compound meaning "fair rose".

SENARA
The latinized name of the patron of Zennor. Nothing is known about her.

SIDWELL
Latin SATIVOLA, possibly a latinzation of an Old English name. St. Sidwell is the patron of Laneast church, near Launceston, and of a parish in Exeter. Nothing is known about her. The name occurs in the 16th and 17th centuries as a rare name for Cornish girls.

SOWENA or SOWENNA
D (Pron. "so-WENN-a") Cornish, "success".

SPLANNA
D Cornish, "brighter".

STEREN
D Cornish, "star".

STERENNYK
D Cornish, "little star".

TALWYN
D A Cornish compound meaning "fair brow".

TAMARA
A name from folk-lore. According to Robert Hunt (Popular Romances of the West of England, 1871), TAMARA was a nymph who gave her name to the Tamar.

TAMSYN
The usual medieval feminine diminutive form of THOMAS. Properly THOMASINE, TAMSYN was once a very popular name for Cornish girls. It became less fashionable in the 18th century but still survives in occasional Cornish use. Because of its obsolescence elsewhere, it is now generally regarded as a Cornish name.

TECCA
D Cornish, "fairer".

TEGEN
D Cornish, "ornament", "pretty little thing", etc.

TREGERETH
D (Pron. "tre-GAIR-eth") Cornish, "mercy", "compassion".

TRESSA
D Cornish, "third".

TRUETH
D (Pron. "troo-eth") Cornish, "compassion".

UGHELLA or EWELLA
D (Pron. "yoo-ELL-a") Cornish, "higher", "more exalted".

WENNA
St. Wenn is the name-saint of the parish adjoining St. Columb and is also patron of Morval church. Her name is GWEN, "white/splendid", which also happens to be the first element in GWENDOLYN. Since the abbreviation GWEN is fairly common, latinized WENNA has been preferred.

WHECCA
D Cornish, "sweeter".

WHEGYN
D Cornish, "sweet or dear little one".

WYLMET or WILMOT
A feminine diminutive of WILLIAM. Fairly common in the earlier parish registers. Has been revived in this century.

YA
(Pron. "ee-a") The name of the saint who gave her name to St. Ives, formerly PORTH YA, "Ya's port".

YGERNA or IGERNA
A name from Arthurian legend. The wife of Gorlois, Duke of Cornwall, and mother of Arthur.

YSELKLA
D (Pron. "iz-ZELL-a") Cornish, "more modest/unpretentious".

+ZENOBIA
The name of a famous queen of Palmyra. For some reason it came into use in late 16th century Cornwall. It may still survive. Occurs as ZONOBY in some parish registers. SINEY seems to be a pet-form of the name.